EXCELLING IN
SOCCER

By Donna B. McKinney

ReferencePoint
Press®

San Diego, CA

© 2020 ReferencePoint Press, Inc.
Printed in the United States

For more information, contact:
ReferencePoint Press, Inc.
PO Box 27779
San Diego, CA 92198
www.ReferencePointPress.com

LIBRARY OF CONGRESS CATALOGING-IN-PUBLICATION DATA

Name: McKinney, Donna B., author.
Title: Excelling in Soccer/by Donna B. McKinney.
Description: San Diego, CA: ReferencePoint Press, Inc., [2020] | Series: Teen Guide to Sports | Audience: Grade 9 to 12 | Includes bibliographical references and index.
ISBN: 978-1-68282-703-1 (hardback)
ISBN: 978-1-68282-704-8 (ebook)
The complete Library of Congress record is available at www.loc.gov.

CONTENTS

INTRODUCTION   4
The Most Popular Sport in the World

CHAPTER 1   10
How Do I Make the Soccer Team?

CHAPTER 2   28
How Do I Get My Body Ready for the Game?

CHAPTER 3   42
How Do I Mentally Prepare for the Game?

CHAPTER 4   56
How Do I Take My Game to the Next Level?

Source Notes	70
For Further Research	74
Index	76
Image Credits	79
About the Author	80

THE MOST POPULAR SPORT
IN THE WORLD

Soccer—or football, as most of the world outside the United States calls it—is the most popular sport in the world. There are millions of soccer players at many skill levels across the globe. Some are brand new to the game and are just learning the basics. Others have played for a while and want to take their skills to the next level. And a few elite professionals play the game at the highest level. But no matter a player's skill level, there are basic guidelines to help him or her improve physically and mentally. By working on parts of their game ranging from drills and nutrition to strategy and teamwork, soccer players can push themselves to the next level.

A game that looks a little bit like modern-day soccer was played in the second and third centuries BCE in China.

> **"I'm attracted to soccer's capacity for beauty. When well played, the game is a dance with a ball."[2]**
>
> – Eduardo Galeano, Uruguayan journalist

All around the world, people love soccer. Whether it's called soccer or football, it has more fans than any other sport.

Tsu' Chu was the name of the Chinese game, which involved kicking a leather ball into a net. Players could use their bodies but not their hands. The modern game of soccer traces its roots to 1863, when the Football Association was formed in England. The Football Association was soccer's first governing body.

THE BEAUTIFUL GAME

Soccer is known as "the beautiful game."[1] Brazilian soccer superstar Pelé used the phrase in his memoir, which was titled *My Life and the Beautiful Game: The Autobiography of Soccer's Greatest Star.* Eduardo Galeano, a Uruguayan journalist and poet who also loved the game of soccer, said, "I'm attracted to soccer's capacity for beauty. When well played, the game is a dance with a ball."[2] Retired English

Players need to sharpen their skills and their minds to get better at soccer. Being able to shoot and pass well won't help players if they don't know where to go.

soccer player David Beckham, who played for Manchester United, said, "Soccer is a magical game."[3] Maybe people think of soccer as a beautiful, magical game because it is so simple. All a player really needs to play the game is a ball. Having cleats, shin guards, and goals can be helpful, but they are not necessary.

Soccer is a sport that enjoys strong popularity around the globe. More than 40 percent of people surveyed from North and South America, Europe, the Middle East, and Asia call themselves soccer fans. Basketball comes in second with 36 percent. Soccer's popularity shows up in the biggest way when the World Cup tournament is played every four years. In this tournament, soccer's biggest event, the teams represent entire nations. Some countries—including Brazil, Germany, and Italy—have proven themselves to be consistent winners in the World Cup. But soccer is a game where even the smaller countries—like Senegal, Ghana, Costa Rica, and Iceland—field national teams and have proven themselves to be highly competitive in World Cup matches.

The game's popularity in the United States is evident too. Approximately 2.3 million children ages six to twelve played soccer in 2018. Spectators in the United States enjoy the game too. The average weekly attendance at Major League Soccer (MLS) matches was around 25,000 in 2018.

The basics of soccer make the game easy enough for children to start playing at a very young age, with many communities offering organized soccer programs for children as young as three or four years old. Soccer can easily be played by adults in recreational leagues too. Fans can enjoy soccer in many ways throughout their lives.

BODY AND MIND BENEFITS

Soccer is also good for both the body and the mind. With the shifts between sprinting, walking, and running, soccer improves a player's cardiovascular health and endurance. It also boosts a player's coordination and speed. And it lowers body fat while improving muscle tone. There are also mental benefits, such as learning to think and react quickly. And soccer helps build the habits of thinking about teamwork and team goals ahead of one's personal goals.

A person who is already playing soccer likely understands the ways it is good for body and mind. For the player who is ready to take his or her game to the next level, there is a whole world of soccer to be explored.

STEPPING UP A PLAYER'S GAME

The first step is working to make the team. Knowing what is expected and being physically and mentally ready for tryouts can significantly increase the chances of making the team. Whether the goal is to play for a community league, join travel or club teams, or make the high school squad, mastering fundamentals such as passing, receiving, dribbling, and shooting the ball are the foundation of all soccer play.

Getting in good physical shape for soccer is the key to executing any plan on the pitch, as the soccer field is called. Physical workouts, nutrition, and practice routines can help ensure a player's body is operating at its best capacity. To achieve the next step in a player's journey, Alex Morgan, an Olympic gold medalist and World Cup champion who plays for the Orlando Pride, tells players to "keep working even when no one is watching."[4]

> **"Keep working even when no one is watching."**[4]
>
> – Alex Morgan, forward for US national team

Mental preparation is a key part of preparing for a soccer match. Tips from professional players about the ways they help keep themselves positive, confident, and focused on their game are helpful. Strategies for pregame routines, dealing with criticism, and building confidence can help players trust themselves and the work they have put in to prepare for the game.

Looking toward long-term goals helps players better understand what it takes to get to the next level and what it takes to play in college and beyond. Focusing on what players and coaches are looking for, how to get recruited, and the kind of physical and mental skills that are required to compete can help a player prepare for the next level.

"The secret is to believe in your dreams; in your potential that you can be like your star, keep searching, keep believing and don't lose faith in yourself," said Brazilian soccer star Neymar.[5] Making the team is the first step.

CHAPTER ONE

HOW DO I MAKE
THE SOCCER TEAM?

I f players strive to play on any kind of organized soccer team, whether it be a community league, a travel or club team, or their high school team, preparation is key. Athletes should make sure that they are ready when the opportunity comes. Pelé, who was on three World Cup teams, said, "Success is no accident. It is hard work, perseverance, learning, studying, sacrifice and most of all, love of what you are doing or learning to do."[6]

> **"Success is no accident."[6]**
>
> – Pelé, Brazilian soccer player

Landon Donovan would probably suggest that anyone interested in competing on a soccer team start by focusing hard on the basics. Donovan is an American soccer player who spent much of his career with the LA Galaxy. He is considered by some to be the best American player ever. He holds the MLS regular-season record and the US men's national team (USMNT) record for goals and assists. Donovan says, "I think we get too caught up in tactics and formation, and perhaps we're still trying to perfect fundamentals and haven't mastered the basics yet. When you're Argentina, Brazil, and Spain, every young kid knows how to trap the ball, pass the ball, cross the

Players should make sure to have fun while learning to play soccer. If they don't enjoy the sport, it will be hard to improve.

ball, do everything perfectly. We're still getting those things, and I think we're putting the cart before the horse a little bit in [the United States]. I didn't learn much of that until I was in my twenties. So if we just take a step back and work on the basics, the rest will come."[7]

Playing soccer is more than just skilled footwork, although that is important. The top soccer players combine physical skills, mental strength, fitness, and knowledge of the game to make themselves

"I think we get too caught up in tactics and formation, and perhaps we're still trying to perfect fundamentals and haven't mastered the basics yet."[7]

– Landon Donovan, American soccer player

the best on the pitch. In soccer, there are six basic skills: dribbling, receiving, passing, shooting, tackling, and heading. To prepare to play on any level team, players will want to practice and develop these fundamental skills.

DRIBBLING

Dribbling is the skill a player uses to move and control the ball with his or her feet. The best way to get better at dribbling is through repetition—endless touches on the ball. Work at using all of the foot—outside, inside, bottom of foot, and heel. Practicing dribbling using one foot and then the other allows either foot to be used as needed in a game situation. A player should work to increase his or her speed while dribbling too. Then practice changing speed and changing direction, all while maintaining constant control of the ball.

A player can practice dribbling alone, but it is also important to practice with another person who is working to take the ball away from the player. Dribbling involves not only footwork, but also concentrating on the way a player moves his or her body. Body movement while dribbling can help the player balance or help fool an opponent with moves such as fakes.

RECEIVING

When a player is receiving a ball, it will come either in the air or on the ground. When the ball comes on the ground, the player should watch the ball and receive it with his or her foot. The heel should be down and the toe pointed up on the receiving foot. When the ball hits the foot, the player should absorb some of the pass. This is called a soft touch. Once a player receives the ball, he or she should be thinking ahead to the next move—either passing, shooting, or dribbling.

GEAR UP

Compared with some other sports, the gear a soccer player needs is fairly simple. Besides the basic gear, players who play the goalkeeper position also need goalkeeper gloves. Many players also use a bag or backpack to carry their gear. Soccer balls range in size from one to five. Youth players usually use a ball ranging from size three to five. The league decides what size ball will be used, depending on the age-group of the players. For soccer shoes, players can choose between turf shoes and cleats. Be sure to get shoes made for soccer, not just baseball or football cleats. Sometimes the league has requirements about the footwear, so players should be sure to check that before shopping.

Receiving the ball in the air requires a player to focus on the ball in flight, noticing the speed and direction of the ball. At this moment, the player must also be thinking about which part of the body to use in receiving the ball—head, chest, thigh, or foot. Players should remember to use their body like a cushion. They should move with the ball or give with the ball a little to receive it with a soft touch. This keeps the ball from bouncing hard off the body and to the other team.

To practice receiving, two players can start simply, taking turns passing and receiving the ball. Players can practice receiving it in the air by tossing the ball to each other. Then, to improve players' skills, add a defender to the drill. The defender will pressure the player to receive the ball quickly and cleanly.

PASSING

Most players like to pass using the inside of the foot. But a player should work on passing using all the parts of the foot. Beyond the foot mechanics involved in passing, a player will also want to work on awareness of where opponents are on the field. Players should note if the opponent has the speed to intercept the pass. Communicating with teammates helps, so a player should not be shy about talking to them. Players should alert teammates to nearby opponents.

Similar to the way he or she practices receiving, a player can practice passing by simply passing and receiving the ball with another player. To make it more complex, practice passing with several players and add in an opponent or two. Opponents can attempt to steal the pass or steal the ball when it is being received. Speed up the practice passes, moving as quickly as possible to simulate the game experience.

SHOOTING

When shooting, a player uses the same skills and techniques developed in passing. But when shooting, the player tries to kick the ball beyond the goalkeeper and into the goal. A player shoots by making contact with the inside of the foot with the foot pointed downward. A player plants one foot beside the ball and swings the other foot forward, making contact with the ball. Be aware of the goalkeeper's position and aim the shot for the gap where the goalkeeper is not standing. When striking the ball, the player should watch the ball as his or her foot strikes it.

To improve shooting, a player can begin by practicing shots on an unguarded goal. Then work on shooting with a goalkeeper guarding the goal. Next add in a defender to help develop strategies for moving around a defender and shooting. Players can also practice shooting using smaller practice goals. These trimmed-down versions are useful in training, helping sharpen a player's accuracy. When faced with

There are many drills to get better at scoring goals. Players should start by shooting at an empty goal.

the decision to pass or shoot, some players prefer to pass instead of taking a shot. Players should not be afraid to take the shot if they are in the right place to take it.

TACKLING

The goal of tackling is to take the ball away from the opponent. But a player needs to be sure to not hurt the opponent while taking the ball away. Players must always remember to go after the ball, not the opponent. Hitting the player instead of the ball could lead to a foul. To tackle successfully, players need to position themselves a couple feet away from the opponent. Players should keep an eye on the ball. Sometimes the player's close presence alone is pressure enough to cause the opponent to make a dribbling or passing error, allowing a player to get a foot on the ball and move it out of the opponent's possession. Bending the knees gives a lower center of gravity and more power as a player moves in to try and take the ball. It also helps the player react more quickly to the opponent's moves. A player should show confidence when tackling, not approaching the opponent in a half-hearted attempt to gain the ball.

HEADING

A player can use his or her head to direct the ball. This move is called a header. Players make contact with the ball on their forehead in the space between the eyebrows and hairline. A player can head the ball in offensive play, working to score a goal, or in defensive play, working to clear the ball into the air and away from an opponent. Heading is a part of the game of soccer. But players should be wise about how they use heading because of the dangers related to head injuries, such as concussions. US Soccer issued guidelines in 2016 that banned heading for children under ten years during practice or games. And US Soccer limits the amount of heading in practices for children eleven to thirteen years old. To be sure players are heading in the proper and safest way possible, they should be sure to follow the instruction of a trained coach as they practice heading.

DEVELOP ALL THE SKILLS

Working on both ball handling skills and shooting skills is essential. Harry Kane, a striker for Tottenham Hotspur in the English Premier League and captain of England's national team, stresses that even players known for their ability to score experience scoring droughts. To ensure that players can keep contributing to the team, it is

Although soccer is not usually considered to be a contact sport, there can be risks for concussions, a type of brain injury. These brain injuries usually occur when a player is heading the ball or when two players collide. In 2018, researchers determined that heading may be riskier for female players than for male players, because females experience more changes in their brain tissue after repetitively heading the ball. To be safe, US Soccer has banned heading for children under ten years. It recommends that players eleven and twelve years old not use heading during practice. The Centers for Disease Control and Prevention (CDC) has created a program called "HEADS UP" to help educate young athletes and their parents about concussions. The program provides information describing symptoms and instructing athletes in what to do if they think they might have a concussion. Any type of brain injury can be serious, so it is important for athletes to learn about concussions and the risks involved. Athletes can find more information about the CDC HEADS UP program on the CDC's website.

important to focus on all aspects of the game. "All goal scorers go on droughts," says Kane. "It is how you cope with that. And it is not just about scoring, it is about what you bring to the team, bringing others into play and getting assists."[8]

ONLY ONE SPORT OR MORE?

Players might wonder if they should narrow their focus to just playing soccer or continue to engage in a variety of sports as they get older. American soccer legend Mia Hamm advises players to enjoy lots of different sports. Hamm led the United States to a gold medal at the 1996 and 2004 Olympic Games and first place in the 1991 and 1999 World Cups. In 2012, ESPN named her the greatest female athlete

Players should watch professional and national team players in games. They can learn by watching how better athletes play the game.

of the past 40 years. Hamm said, "I didn't specialize until I made the national team. I still played basketball and a bunch of different sports, really kind of followed what my friends were playing in the season that was being organized. I think that helped me not burn out so early and helped my overall athleticism."[9]

Joshua Smith, an American player who plays for SC Hessen Dreieich, a German soccer club, makes the same point as Hamm about the importance of playing a variety of sports. "I played basketball until my junior year," he said. "I played baseball a lot when I was younger; I ran cross-country and track. I'd say I was pretty good at basketball, might even have potentially started on the varsity team as a point guard. But I realized pretty soon that soccer could actually take me somewhere."[10] Smith said playing point guard in basketball helped his soccer game because the point guard is like a midfielder, but with a smaller playing area.

BUILDING A STRONG ATTITUDE

While preparing physically for team tryouts, players should also spend some time focusing on mental strength. Keep focused on what is happening on the field, even during drills and practice scrimmages. Players should work to improve awareness of where teammates and opponents are at all times. Play with confidence, realizing that everyone makes mistakes at times. Letting a mistake lead to another mistake or a penalty hurts the team.

Hamm was wildly successful as a soccer player at the high school, national, and international levels. Yet she understood that even the best players make mistakes and experience failure at times. "Failure happens all the time," she said. "It happens every day in practice. What makes you better is how you react to it."[11]

High school players can learn by watching the best soccer players in professional games. They should watch how the pros move on the

> "Failure happens all the time. It happens every day in practice. What makes you better is how you react to it."[11]
>
> – Mia Hamm, American soccer player

Teams have eleven players on the pitch. How they are arranged is up to the coach.

field, with and without the ball. Think about what they are doing as they move with the ball, set up scoring opportunities, move without the ball, and defend against a potent offense. High school players can analyze the strategy involved in the way they play, and then work to put that into practice. Players also watch their peers, noting what these players at their level are doing right and wrong. Studying the positive and negative aspects of other players' games can be a way for players to improve their own play.

JUST THE RULES

Along with developing ball handling skills and mental strength, players want to be sure they are familiar with the rules of the game. The National Federation of State High School Associations (NFHS) sets the rules for high school sports, including soccer. Players can find details about the rules of high school soccer, along with any changes to the rules that might occur year to year, at the NFHS website.

The NFHS gives some basic rules for soccer. It recommends the high school field be 100 yards (91 m) by 65 yards (59 m) in size. The field markings for the penalty area, the goal, and touch lines are the same markings that Fédération Internationale de Football Association (FIFA) uses. High school teams use a size 5 soccer ball, which is considered an adult-size ball. It is the ball size usually recommended for players thirteen and older.

Each team fields eleven players, including the goalkeeper. Each team has a person designated as the captain. High school players are required to wear a jersey, shorts, socks, shin guards, and cleats in games. In high school, the game is played with two forty-minute periods or four twenty-minute quarters, along with a ten-minute overtime if needed. Individual state high school athletic associations can decide to use a twenty-minute overtime or a sudden death victory extra time. At the college and professional levels, the game has two forty-five-minute halves plus the stoppage time. Since the clock runs without stopping during the game, the referee adds stoppage time on to the end of the game to make up for any pauses that occurred during the regular game time. There is usually one main referee and two assistant referees. Sometimes there is a fourth official who monitors substitutions. The referee also holds the yellow and red cards. The referee raises a card to signal that a player has broken the rules. A yellow card is a warning for breaking a rule. A red card is for a more serious rule violation, and the player who committed the violation must leave the field. The team cannot substitute another player into the game after this, so they are forced to play down one player, with only ten players on the field.

POSITIONS IN SOCCER

The United States National Soccer Team Players Association defines four basic positions in the game of soccer. They are goalkeeper, defender, midfielder, and forward. Each position requires a different skill set and a different type of player. Each team has one goalkeeper. This player, often called a keeper, is positioned in front of the goal, and his or her one main job is to keep the other team from scoring. Goalkeepers are the only players on the field allowed to touch the ball with their hands in the field of play. Inside the goal box, the box marked on the field around the goal, goalkeepers can use their hands to stop or catch the ball. Once they stop or catch a ball in play, goalkeepers can kick to clear the ball out of the area and as far away from their goal as possible. They can also throw the ball to a teammate. Goalkeepers wear a shirt that is a different color from their teammates' jerseys, so the referee can easily see which player is the goalkeeper.

It is common for teams to play with four defenders on the field. There is flexibility in the game, so coaches can choose to use different formations of players. The defenders are those players positioned on the field in front of the keeper. As the position's name suggests, the defenders work to defend the goal. They try to keep the ball from getting past them headed toward their goalkeeper. Depending on where the coach positions the defenders on the field, they might have more specific names like center back, sweeper, fullback, or wingback.

Teams commonly play with four midfielders on the field. The midfielders typically play both offensive and defensive roles in a game. They help the defenders keep the other team from scoring. They also work to push the ball up the field to the forwards, so that the forwards have a chance to score. The midfielders sometimes get opportunities

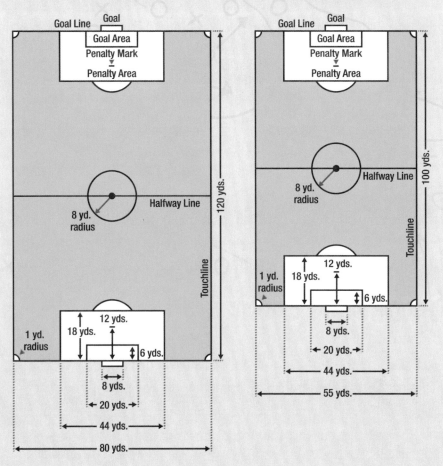

FIFA

Goal Line · Goal
Goal Area
Penalty Mark
Penalty Area
Halfway Line
8 yd. radius
120 yds.
Touchline
12 yds.
18 yds.
1 yd. radius
6 yds.
8 yds.
20 yds.
44 yds.
80 yds.

HIGH SCHOOL

Goal Line · Goal
Goal Area
Penalty Mark
Penalty Area
8 yd. radius
Halfway Line
100 yds.
Touchline
12 yds.
18 yds.
1 yd. radius
6 yds.
8 yds.
20 yds.
44 yds.
55 yds.

Soccer fields are different sizes. In high school most fields are the same size. With faster professional players, the field needs to be bigger. In FIFA games, the field is longer and wider. No matter the competition level, penalty boxes should remain the same size. Larger goals would make scoring too easy.

to score themselves. At the start of a game, the midfielders are positioned in front of the defenders and behind the forwards. During the flow of game action, they move around on the field a lot, but they mostly play in the center area of the field. Like the defenders, they might have more specific names depending on where they line up on the field. These might be names like center midfielder, defensive midfielder, attacking midfielder, or wide midfielder, also called winger.

It is common for a team to play with two forwards on the field. They are sometimes called strikers. The forwards' job is to score goals. At the start of the game, the forwards line up at the midfield line. Most of their time on the field is played between that midfield line and the opposing team's goal. The forwards might also have more specific names like center forward, second striker, or winger.

TRY DIFFERENT POSITIONS

As players gain more experience in playing soccer, they should not limit themselves to practicing and learning just one position. By trying different positions, players may find that they are better at a certain position. They might miss this if they limit themselves to playing a single position. Learning other positions can also help a player better understand the game and the position he or she prefers.

Kevin Nicholson, a coach with Cardiff City FC U-23 team in the Premier League, stresses this idea. "Coaches should encourage players to try playing in a number of different positions on the field," he said. "This will help young players

> **"I worked on my weaknesses and made them my strengths."**[13]
>
> *– Sydney Leroux, professional soccer player for the Orlando Pride and the US women's national team*

Coaches ask players to change positions based on their skills. Players can learn new parts of the game this way.

broaden their experience of the game. It's good for them to be in different areas of the pitch when playing a match—it's certainly very different playing right back than it is playing in central midfield."[12]

TACKLING THE TRYOUTS

No matter the skill level in soccer, consistent practice will help a player improve. Sydney Leroux has won a gold medal and a World Cup in soccer and currently plays for the Orlando Pride. "I worked on my weaknesses and made them my strengths," she said.[13] Whether players are trying to make the team for the first time or gain more playing time, working to improve any weaknesses is key. Turning particular weaknesses into strengths can be a player's goal as he or she prepares for team tryouts.

Every player needs to dribble and pass. Drills can help sharpen these skills.

For most high school teams, the tryouts take place over the course of several days. Nate Hetherington coaches the boys' soccer teams at Cathedral Catholic High School in San Diego, California. Hetherington said he runs his team tryouts in what he describes as a pretty standard setup. He starts tryouts with warm-ups and stretching. Next up, he says, "I run players though different quick passing drills. Lots of one-touch passing and ball control. After that, I leave a lot of time for small-sided scrimmages." Small-sided scrimmages are typically four-on-four games played in a small area with practice goals.

These scrimmages are key. "The small-sided scrimmages," he says, "give me the best chance to observe each player's style, skill, soccer brain, and mentality."[14]

Mike Jones, coach at Horizon Prep in California, offers this advice to players: "Smile. A positive attitude is so important and will keep a coach's attention at tryouts. Don't complain. Ever. Work hard. No excuses. You'll make mistakes. Everyone makes mistakes, even the best players. The great thing about this game is when you mess up, there's always a time in the near future for you to make up for it."[15]

"You'll make mistakes. Everyone makes mistakes, even the best players. The great thing about this game is when you mess up, there's always a time in the near future for you to make up for it."[15]

– Mike Jones, head coach at Horizon Prep in California

CHAPTER TWO

HOW DO I GET MY BODY READY FOR THE GAME?

When it comes to training and getting in shape for soccer, having a plan will help any player. Jimmy Conrad played MLS soccer for thirteen years with the San Jose Earthquakes, Kansas City Wizards, and Chivas USA. In 2005, he was honored as the MLS Defender of the Year. Conrad also played for the USMNT between 2005 and 2010. He majored in mathematics while playing college soccer for the University of California, Los Angeles. Conrad said he never went to the park to play with no thought or plan for what he was doing. "I always had a plan," he said.[16] One day he would work on his left foot. The next day he might work on two-touch passing. Another day he might work on long ball kicks. The next day he might work on

> "So having really determined and purposeful training makes a big difference. I'm always surprised how people really don't think about the structure of how they are training. They just go out there and run around for 30 minutes without really having a plan. I think you really need a plan because it keeps you focused."[17]
>
> – Jimmy Conrad, retired American soccer player

Soccer requires that players be in good shape. Fitness includes strength, speed, endurance, and flexibility.

trapping the ball. Conrad's plan involved working on all aspects of his game.

"These little things matter and I try to practice the little things as much as possible," Conrad said. "So having really determined and purposeful training makes a big difference. I'm always surprised how people really don't think about the structure of how they are training. They just go out there and run around for thirty minutes without really having a plan. I think you really need a plan because it keeps you focused."[17]

PHYSICAL CONDITIONING

Running is a key part of soccer. Players in World Cup competition run approximately 7 miles (11 km) in a game. Chasing a ball over a large field makes the miles add up quickly. Players at the midfielder position run the most. Midfielders run an estimated 9.5 miles (15 km) in a game.

Many players in the Premier League regularly use interval training to increase their conditioning and endurance. Interval training is alternating between two activities that require different rates of speed, like short bursts of intense activity and then longer times of less strenuous activity. Players may sprint at high speed and then jog and then sprint again. A good drill for this might be four minutes of jogging and then four minutes of running, repeated several times.

Sprinting speed is important for players at any position on the soccer field, so it is important for players to work on drills that increase their speed. Use of resistance drills such as sled sprints, parachute sprints, or hill sprints can help increase a player's ability to accelerate and run fast for short distances. Hill sprints should be performed after warming up. They consist of four rounds of fifteen-second sprints up a hill. The increased strain of running up the hill will require a larger amount of strength than running on a level surface. Players should also make sure to run upright and keep their strides short when running uphill. Keeping the hips below the shoulders and not leaning forward helps the legs deliver more power on each stride. Smaller strides help keep each stride compact and powerful. Sled sprints use a small sled that holds weightlifting weights. The athlete pushes the loaded sled back and forth in short bursts. This helps increase

Soccer is a quick-paced, fast-moving game. Even referees with the sharpest eyes might sometimes struggle to see whether or not the ball has crossed the goal line. Now, using goal-line technology, sensors track the movement of the ball and players to determine if the ball crosses all of the goal line. This technology is accurate to within 0.03 inches (0.8 mm). When a player shoots at the goal, match officials receive a message on their watches telling them whether or not the whole ball has crossed the goal line. This technology must not interfere with the flow of the game, so the information is sent to the officials' watches within one second. Goal-line technology was introduced during the 2014 World Cup in Brazil. It was also used in the 2018 World Cup in Russia.

speed and explosive leg strength. Parachute sprints are similar to sled sprints. Instead of pushing a weighted sled, the athlete runs with a parachute dragging behind them. The air resistance offered by the parachute makes the short sprints harder.

BUILDING BODY STRENGTH

Besides the focus on running and sprinting, a soccer player should work on developing body strength too. "Strength is a quality that underpins everything," says Jordan Webb, a strength and conditioning coach for the University of Notre Dame. Before coming to Notre Dame, Webb was a strength and conditioning coach for the Chicago Fire. "It underpins endurance, agility, speed—it underpins power production, everything you need to be an athlete. I think that body strength is probably the quality that is most important for any soccer player, no matter the position."[18]

Webb says soccer players sometimes neglect working on their upper- and lower-body strength. They are putting themselves at a disadvantage when they do this. "Some players have a tendency to put [strength training] off to the side," he says.[19] Webb uses a variety of exercises with the athletes he works with—lower body pushing, front and back squats, different styles of deadlifts, different bench presses, dumbbell rows, push presses, and pull-downs.

Webb points to the star of the Italian professional club Juventus. "Look at [Cristiano] Ronaldo—that guy is an absolute athletic specimen," he says. "There's a certain level of strength and fitness that you need, and the most important thing is getting an adequate level of strength."[20] General weight training is important in helping players prevent injuries. A regular weekly routine of deadlifts, squats, and lunges helps players improve their overall strength.

Strengthening the core—those muscles in the abdomen, back, and pelvis—increases a player's flexibility, endurance, and stamina.

"The core is extremely important for players, glute strength, lower body strength, and hip mobility are important—a strong core helps add power and prevent injuries."[21]

– Paul Caffrey, sports performance director and fitness coach for the Houston Dynamo

Paul Caffrey is the sports performance director and fitness coach for the Houston Dynamo in the MLS. "For me," he says, "the core is extremely important for players, glute strength, lower body strength, and hip mobility are important—a strong core helps add power and prevent injuries." He adds, "We do a lot of work on hip mobility and hip strength, because there's a lot of muscles that are connecting together—they need to be strong for players to run as much as they do. If you have tight hips, then you will be less mobile, you'll be less functional, less powerful."[21]

Caffrey suggests three exercises that can help players add strength to their core and lower body. Dumbbell lunges using weights help a player improve lower body balance and stability while also improving running speed. Weighted step-ups, where players hold dumbbells at their side and step up onto a box or bench, strengthen the legs and lower body while also improving running and jumping. Goblet squats, where players hold a dumbbell or kettlebell while standing and squatting, strengthen both the legs and core. There are many more exercises for the core too. Planks are a great exercise for the core. Players assume a position close to a pushup, but lower so that they rest on the elbow. Players should maintain a straight back and flat shoulders and hold for thirty seconds. The body should resemble a straight plank from the shoulders to the feet.

PRACTICE ROUTINES AND TRAINING

When practicing with a team, players should work to get maximum benefit from the practice time. This means a player gives his or her best effort, listens and follows the coach's instructions, and strives to make improvements with every practice. A strong mental attitude is important at practice too. Players can encourage teammates and not get discouraged over the mistakes that will happen.

Practicing with a plan in mind helps a player see quicker improvements in his or her game. Alex Morgan says, "I set goals for myself every month, specific things I want to work on each month. I go out by myself, or with teammates after training and do specific shooting drills, long balls, one-v-one—whatever it is I need to work on.

As a soccer player, I'm always developing and continuing to improve myself."[22]

SOLO PRACTICE

For the player who wants to put in more work apart from the team practices, there are some solo drills that can help improve skills. A wall can provide a good training partner for a player to practice trapping skills. A player kicks the ball hard off the wall, either low or high, and then traps the ball as it returns from the wall. Practice kicking and trapping with both feet to maximize ball handling abilities.

A player can also work on solo drills using cones. Work on dribbling and weaving around the cones, similar to the drills done in a team practice. Players should keep the ball close to their bodies and focus on ball control as they dribble. Again, work to improve with both feet.

Shooting is another skill a player can work on alone. Attempt shots from different distances and different locations in front of the goal. Christen Press, who plays for the National Women's Soccer League (NWSL) Utah Royals FC and US national team, really focused on her shooting as a younger player. "You can ask anyone that I've ever played with or talked to," she says. "I'm an obsessive shooter. I go out and shoot all the time. I used to take 200 shots every single day—it's something that I started with my mom. In the Pelé videos I would

COOPER TEST

Some soccer coaches use the Cooper Test as part of the team tryouts. This running test was developed by Dr. Kenneth Cooper in 1968 while he was working for the US Air Force. Across the years, athletes in a wide range of sports have endured this twelve-minute run. The object is for athletes to finish as many laps on a standard 400-meter high school track as possible in twelve minutes. The number of laps completed is a measure of the maximum oxygen consumption by an athlete during vigorous exercise. Female varsity high school runners can usually complete about seven to eight laps, while males can complete about eight to nine laps. The Cooper Test is a simple way for coaches to assess an athlete's fitness level. Some coaches use it at tryouts and then over time to see how athletes' fitness levels are improving with training. Both sports teams and the military continue using the Cooper Test today, more than fifty years after it was invented.

watch, he used to line up 10 balls and shoot them in a row—so I did that exercise all the way through college."[23]

TRY ANOTHER SPORT IN THE OFF-SEASON

Another way for soccer players to think about training is to consider the sports they play in their off-season. Working out and staying active year-round can help a player stay in top shape for the soccer season. Nick Harvey is a physical performance coach for English soccer clubs such as Southampton Academy, Reading FC, and England's U21 men's team. When asked what he would recommend for a soccer player looking to play other sports, Harvey named team sports first because of the similarities as far as training and decision-making.

In addition to team sports, Harvey says, "Sports that I quite like, like combat sports, stuff like judo, things like that, can help with the grappling skills and the combat skills. Being able to control your

Weightlifting is a key component to a player's overall strength. Lifting with correct form is key to safely performing the exercises.

body weight and working against somebody else's body weight. They're good for also teaching some discipline as well, so that would be a couple of examples."[24] Harvey also likes tennis and racquetball because of the demands on coordination and how different they are from soccer. Playing a sport that moves the body differently helps reduce burnout too.

PRO PLAYERS' TRAINING ROUTINES

So what might a training routine look like for a professional soccer player? Professional players need bodies that can run about seven miles per game and last for 90-minute matches. Amy Rodriguez, who plays for the Utah Royals FC and the US Women's National Team (USWNT), describes her training routines this way: "I train just about every day, and sometimes I train twice a day. My training consists of soccer practice, weight lifting, agility, and speed work. I like to have one day off a week so my body can rest and recover."[25]

"Fitness is a huge part of our game," says Alex Morgan. "It is difficult to go out there by yourself and do, you know, forty-five minutes straight with no one watching, no one holding you accountable; but to get to this level you need to hold yourself accountable and you need to be able to put in this work, *especially* when no one's watching. When we're outside of National Team training camps, we are kind of on our own. I'm in the gym weight lifting two to three times a week, and then you either need to find a team or a few players."[26] Having a teammate to practice and work out with can help keep a player accountable to his or her training plan.

NUTRITION

Rodriguez stresses the importance of smart, healthy eating. "It's really important that I eat healthy while I'm playing soccer," she says. "In order to have energy for the games, I need to make sure I'm putting the right foods in my body. Things like whole grain carbs, protein, fruits and veggies are what I strive to eat on a daily basis."[27] This means not just smart eating on game day, but choosing healthy foods every day.

For an athlete at any level, healthy eating is a must. But there is more to it than just eating good foods and avoiding bad foods. Knowing what kinds of foods to eat and when to eat them can aid an athlete's preparation. Chris Ina is the athletic training coordinator in the Wake Forest Baptist Medical Center sports medicine department. Ina says, "Parents, young athletes and coaches should know that one of the most important elements of proper nutrition for sports is timing.

In addition to eating balanced meals, young athletes need to know when to eat what types of food so they allow enough time for proper digestion and absorption of the nutrients needed for performance 'fuel.'"[28] In the days leading up to a game, a player should eat plenty of carbohydrates. Choose from foods like baked potatoes, peanut butter, applesauce, spaghetti with tomato sauce, low-fat yogurt, pancakes with syrup, bananas, skim milk, fruit juices, bagels, and whole-grain pastas or breads.

Before the game, avoid big meals that take hours to digest. A small meal eaten two to four hours before the game or heavy practice is wise. This meal should be high in carbohydrates and low in fat and protein. Avoid spicy foods, high-fiber foods, or foods that cause gas at this meal. Also steer clear of carbonated drinks. If players are hungry before the game or practice, they should eat smart with a small snack about an hour before the event starts. University of Rochester sports dietitian Gina Giannetti suggests the following pregame snacks: a peanut butter sandwich, trail mix, fruit, or apple slices with peanut butter.

Game-day drinks can include low-fat or skim milk and fruit juices up to two hours before the game or practice. In the two hours before the game or practice, players should choose water and sports drinks. They should steer clear of carbonated drinks and drinks with caffeine, such as coffee, tea, or cola. After games or hard practices, athletes are usually hungry and ready to refuel. For a quick snack, trail mix, a banana, and a sports drink or low-fat chocolate milk are good choices.

Sometimes in tournaments, players might find themselves playing more than one game in a day. If there are more than two hours between games, then players can eat a light meal. With less than two

Lean meats are the best sources of protein. They help provide a healthy and balanced meal too.

hours, a small, high-carb snack along with water or a sports drink is best. High-carb snacks include graham crackers, pretzels, oatmeal raisin cookies, low-fat puddings or yogurt, saltine crackers, or raisins.

In general, athletes should avoid fried, greasy food, such as cheeseburgers and fries. Working to digest the fat leaves a player's body feeling sluggish. And while the occasional sweets—such as candy, cookies, and chocolate-covered granola bars—are okay, athletes should try to make healthy food choices the main part of their diet. Young athletes should give their diet the same thought and attention they give to their physical workouts and practices. "The energy requirements needed for the sustained physical activity involved in practice and competitive sports are much higher than for normal, day-to-day activities," says Giannetti.[29]

Players should stick to water or sports drinks during games. These drinks help rehydrate players.

HYDRATION

Hydration—drinking enough water—is important for athletes. Even when an athlete might not feel thirsty, he or she still could be needing fluids. With all the running involved in a practice or game, Giannetti says athletes should drink 8 ounces (0.24 L) of water or sports drink every twenty to thirty minutes. And don't wait till practice or game time to think about hydration. Players need to drink plenty of water throughout the day before a practice or game starts. Giannetti recommends a formula for determining how much water an athlete needs. Players should weigh themselves before and after a heavy practice or game. For every pound lost, an athlete should drink

32 ounces (0.95 L) of water to replace what was lost. They should drink this much water over the course of the next heavy practice or game.

Sports drinks are helpful in replenishing the parts of sweat that are more than just water. Things like electrolytes need to be replenished too. But these drinks also contain a lot of sugar. Players should monitor the amount of sugar they ingest from sports drinks. In most situations water will work, but in games and in hot weather, the added benefits of these drinks can help.

WHAT ABOUT SUPPLEMENTS?

Some athletes take protein supplements in addition to the food they eat. After a game or practice, a supplement bar or shake can be an option if other foods are not easily available. "Remember that supplements don't replace a good diet or the workouts you need," Giannetti cautions. "I see a lot of athletes take too many supplements, thinking they'll boost performance, but only end up putting on unwanted weight."[30] With a balanced diet, athletes should be able to get all the protein they need from food. Good, lean protein sources include chicken, turkey, fish, pork, eggs, nuts, Greek yogurt, hummus, and milk. The most important things are to eat a balance of good food and to work hard.

CHAPTER THREE

HOW DO I MENTALLY PREPARE
FOR THE GAME?

A person's mental attitude affects every area of life—not just in sports, but in the classroom, in relationships, and in jobs. Kelsee Pottorff played soccer for the University of California, Irvine, where she was majoring in psychology and social behavior, with a plan to pursue law or other careers involving public service. Pottorff offers this advice to the next generation of girls playing soccer: "Challenge yourselves to be the best version of yourself that you can be, not only as soccer players, but as people." She adds, "Stay true to yourself and your beliefs and remain confident in who you are. Soccer players are all unique in their own way. As people, take pride in your individuality. Be confident in who you are and what makes you who you truly are. Find what motivates you and use that to challenge yourself on a daily basis in all the areas of your life."[31]

MENTAL TOUGHNESS

While it might be easy for a coach to observe and measure a soccer player's physical traits, the player's mental strength might be harder to measure. However, scientists are working to better understand how a soccer player's mental ability impacts his or her ability to succeed in the sport. Sports researchers at the University of Lincoln and

Playing with confidence is key. It can help a player take the shot rather than pass the ball.

Liverpool John Moores University in the United Kingdom conducted a study to understand the psychological qualities required for a player to rise to the top levels of professional soccer. They interviewed coaches from an English Premier League soccer academy to explore the idea of "mental toughness" and why top players seem to possess this toughness.

Sports psychologist Dan Abrahams recommends that soccer players at any level of competition have a "script" that they focus on before every game. This script consists of several actions the player wants to achieve during the game. For example, a script might be something like this: "Always be on my toes. Keep my head up and find space. Track my man at all times, and don't stop moving. Be brave with the ball and take players on. Always fill the space."

Before the game, Abrahams encourages players to mentally rehearse their script and even picture themselves executing it. Then, during warm-ups, players can talk to themselves, recalling their script and encouraging themselves with their own thoughts and words. While rehearsing the script does not guarantee a player success during the actual game, Abrahams feels it gives the player a great chance to succeed. "You can only be the best that you can be," Abrahams says. "You can't force a great performance so relax, calm, chill—let your performance take care of itself. Just stick to your script with relentless enthusiasm and the outcome will take care of itself." And knowing that mistakes do happen and bad games come along, players can encourage themselves with this kind of reminder: "I'm going to play my best game. If I don't, I will correct it for the next game."

Dan Abrahams, "Preparing to Play–a Mental Warm Up," Amplified Soccer, March 28, 2016. www.amplifiedsoccerathlete.com.

The researchers discovered that "mentally tough players demonstrated a commitment to learning, had a strong level of trust with their coach, were more compliant with instructions and were always seeking ways to improve."[32] These successful players who were mentally tough had learned how to deal with criticism and were able to keep going after repeated failures. They did not let other people intimidate them. The researchers say these mentally tough players "were not afraid to make mistakes, and actually relished challenging situations; they were committed to learning how to cope with their own limitations by working on weaknesses whilst also playing to strengths."[33] On the opposite side, the researchers discovered that "young players who were high maintenance, requiring a lot of supervision, support, or relying on others to solve their problems were less likely to make it to the top of their profession."[34]

Players echo what the researchers describe—that mental toughness is key. Retired USWNT star Mia Hamm says, "The most important attribute a player must have is mental toughness."[35] Players can practice and work hard to develop strength, quickness, and better ball handling skills. But how do soccer players improve the mental parts of the game? There are strategies for developing mental strength as a player.

STAY COACHABLE

One of the observations the researchers made in studying mentally tough players was that they were committed to learning and they trusted their coach. As a young player, it is important to stay coachable. A player should know that there is always room for her to improve. Trusting the coach to help her improve individually and as part of the team allows for her to grow.

Mentally tough players notice what other players are doing. They don't do this to feel intimidated or wish they had the other players' skills. Instead, they try to learn from those players. They come to practices and games thinking about what they could learn, how they

The best players learn from their mistakes. Talking to a coach can help a player figure out how to fix the problem.

can get better, or how they can support their teammates. Constantly looking for ways to learn and improve in the sport helps keep a player from getting bored with practice and training. It helps him enjoy soccer more and become a better player in the process.

It is also helpful to remember that practice is the key to mastering any sport. There are no shortcuts to success in sports or in life. Players who stay coachable and who are eager to learn will see improvements in their physical game while maintaining a strong mental attitude.

LEARN FROM THE MISTAKES

Learning from failures instead of giving up is another sign of being mentally tough. Players should recognize that mistakes are a part of the learning process, whether they are doing math problems or taking penalty kicks.

Mentally tough players do not let mistakes cause them to think about quitting. They know that the mistakes are a part of the process of becoming a better soccer player. The key is to look at the mistakes, learn from them, and make the adjustments needed to improve. Players should listen to the coach's criticism with a goal of getting better. Ivan Rakitic of FC Barcelona and the Croatian national team says,

> **"The smartest thing I did is I never gave up."[36]**
>
> *– Ivan Rakitic, player for FC Barcelona and the Croatian national team*

"The smartest thing I did is I never gave up."[36] Players who refuse to give up are able to move past mistakes, looking ahead to the next practice or the next game with the confidence that they can learn and improve.

One way to learn from mistakes is to make time for thinking. Mentally tough players spend time thinking about how to better play their position. They visualize themselves succeeding with these skills at practice and in games. These players create mental pictures of the goals they have set for themselves and see themselves reaching their goals.

Players who are mentally tough do not set unrealistic expectations for themselves. Setting small, reachable goals helps a player move quickly along the path toward greater successes. For example, mentally tough players might focus on playing their game well, not just trying to win. They focus on the positive—things they are doing well—and refuse to let negative thinking or frustration get them down.

A good question for players to ask themselves when they make a mistake is, "How can I stay calm and focused?" Asking this question helps a player keep his or her mind ready to learn from the mistake and move forward toward better play.

EMBRACE THE CHALLENGES

The researchers discovered mentally tough players "actually relished challenging situations."[37] Players who allow the coach's criticism or their own mistakes to overwhelm them seldom reach their full potential as a player. They get so discouraged by their mistakes in the past that they miss out on opportunities to play well in the future.

Mentally tough players trust themselves—their practice, their hard work, their skills. They commit to doing whatever it takes to improve as a player. They are willing to put in the hard work at organized practices and in their own time to develop their skills. They listen and learn from the coach's praise and criticism. These players see challenges as opportunities for better play.

Carli Lloyd plays for the NWSL's Sky Blue FC and the USWNT. She has won two Olympic gold medals and a FIFA Women's World Cup championship. Recognizing her excellent play, FIFA named her Player of the Year in 2015 and 2016. Lloyd is a player who put in the hard work to enjoy the success she knows today. Here are her words of advice on how to find success at the highest levels of soccer: "Life is complicated. Life is going to throw all kinds of obstacles in your way. All I can tell you is what works for me: be true to yourself, don't do fake, and above all else, keep on working, because that's what will take you where you want to go."[38]

Carli Lloyd (right) *has worked hard to get where she is. Mental toughness allows her to keep practicing even when her schedule is hectic.*

One important thing to remember is that soccer is a game, and it is supposed to be fun. There was a time when Christen Press did not enjoy the game so much. "I used to be so focused on winning, I had a really hard time enjoying soccer," she says. "If I missed a shot, I would spend a lot of time thinking about how I'd disappointed my teammates. Then I learned how moments of struggle make you stronger."[39] Players who embrace the challenges are able to enjoy

WHAT IS FUTSAL?

Futsal is a fast-paced, indoor version of soccer developed in Brazil and played with five players on each side. It is often played on a hard-surface floor, like a basketball court, using a ball that is smaller and with less bounce than a traditional soccer ball. There is no off-sides in futsal. One of the five players is the goalkeeper, but in futsal, unlike in soccer, the goalkeeper plays very actively on the field. Futsal can be a great game for soccer players wanting to improve their technical skills, because it requires players to react quickly, think fast, be creative, and make pinpoint accurate passes—all skills that transfer well to a player's outdoor soccer game. During a game, players get many touches on the ball and lots of opportunities to score. Futsal is played around the world. The name *futsal* comes from the Portuguese *Futebol de salão*, which translates as "room football." Soccer superstars like Pelé, Cristiano Ronaldo, Lionel Messi, and Ricardo Kaka have played the game since childhood, and they give it credit for helping to develop their soccer skills.

the game and enjoy correcting a mistake. This turns a weakness or failure into a strength. These players usually find greater success along the way.

OVERCOME WEAKNESSES

The researchers also noted that mentally tough players learned "how to cope with their own limitations by working on weaknesses."[40] Players should ask what are their strengths and weaknesses, and where they can improve.

Jimmy Conrad liked to keep a list of goals he set for himself. His list would include realistic things like scoring three goals in a year—things he felt like he could easily achieve. And he would also include big goals that might be more of a challenge to reach.

Conrad also put daily goals on his list, like not making a mistake today or planning how he would handle mistakes he did make. "You are going to feel so bad about yourself sometimes so you have to figure out a way to keep moving forward with learning from the past, but also not letting it anger you," Conrad says. "Your short-term goals should work towards your long-term goals! Personally, I think the guys that are the toughest mentally are the ones that stick around the longest."[41] Setting and completing goals is a great way for players to chart their personal improvement over time. Checking off the goals helps a player see the improvement as they overcome weaknesses and mold them into strengths.

PREGAME ROUTINES

Feeling some stress before a game is to be expected. A little stress can be a good thing. It can help a player focus better and give a boost of adrenaline. But too much stress can overwhelm a player. This causes anxiety and is most definitely not a good thing. To combat the stress and get ready to play, many players follow pregame routines to ensure they manage the jitters and are mentally ready to play.

Some players practice deep breathing exercises, slowly inhaling through the nose and then exhaling slowly through the mouth. They practice this slow, deep breathing for several minutes to help them relax. Other players do light aerobic exercise for relaxation. This could be as simple as walking or jogging at a slow pace. Listening to music helps other players focus and relax before the game. Some players like to visualize game scenarios and imagine themselves playing well. They think about how they would react in certain situations. This helps them react more quickly and with confidence when faced with these situations in an actual game.

Landon Donovan believes he plays his best soccer when he takes care of himself. Taking care of the mind is just as important as taking care of the body.

RELAXING

Landon Donovan, the great USMNT player who spent much of his career with the LA Galaxy, practiced meditation before his games. "I play best when I'm happy inside," says Donovan, "and that comes from me working on myself. When I take care of myself emotionally and physically, I perform better. So success isn't an accident."[42]

Press is another player who uses meditation. "I meditate daily," Press says, "and I think it's sort of a life skill. It's highly applicable on the soccer field: I find the ball and I think, 'Where's the ball going and where do I need to go?' It's the simplest thing, but it's become sort of like my soccer mantra. I simply use the ball as my focus point and move back into position, and the distracting thoughts disappear and I'm right back in the game."[43]

Besides the pregame strategies for combating stress, some players use regular habits to help themselves stay more mentally focused and relaxed. Roy Keane, a former star player for the Premier League's Manchester United, took up yoga to help improve his soccer game. Yoga is an exercise practice that works both the body and the mind. In yoga, participants use stretching, postures, breathing, and meditation. For Keane, yoga was a regular part of his routine, helping him physically and mentally. "There are benefits," Keane says. "You loosen the muscle and take pressure off your joints."[44]

Players who find a game-day routine that works for them often discover that it helps them be mentally prepared and more relaxed, so they can perform their best during the game. Players should find a routine that helps them focus on the game, clear away distractions, and relax. A routine might include team stretches, pregame drills, listening to music, and visualizing the game plan.

DON'T NEGLECT SLEEP

One easy way for athletes to help themselves both mentally and physically is to get enough rest. "Getting enough sleep is crucial for athletic performance," says Dr. David Geier, an orthopedic surgeon and sports medicine specialist.[45] Teens need nine to nine and a half hours of sleep each night, according to Dr. Michael Crocetti, a pediatrician with Johns Hopkins Medicine. For teen athletes, this

Getting enough sleep is very important. Poor sleep can undo the hard work of training and working out.

number is even higher. "Just as athletes need more calories than most people when they're in training, they need more sleep too," says Dr. Geier. "Not getting enough sleep doesn't only make you tired the next day. It has a big impact on what's happening inside your body."[46] Athletes who are training regularly with practices and games should sleep about an extra hour a day, says Jim Thornton, the former president of the National Athletic Trainers' Association. Athletes can gain this extra hour by either going to bed earlier or taking a nap in the afternoon.

A research study conducted on the Stanford University basketball team had the players add an average of almost two extra hours of sleep each night. The research team studied the players over a period of several months. With this extra sleep, the players increased their speed by 5 percent and their free throw accuracy by 9 percent.

Their reflexes were faster, and overall they felt happier. Sleep makes a positive difference. "Sleep is the time when your body repairs itself," says Felicia Stoler, an exercise physiologist and registered dietitian. "If we don't get enough sleep, we don't perform well."[47]

Alex Oxlade-Chamberlain, an English player who competes for the Premier League's Liverpool FC, explains the importance of sleep to his play. "I always try to make sure I get ten hours on the night of the game. Is that a lot? With anything else I'm dead. If it's an evening game, I'll nap. So, ten hours, then a nap."[48]

Soccer players who want to improve their sleep habits should go to bed and get up at the same times each day—a regular sleep schedule is important. Avoid taking any sleep aid medicine, unless a healthcare provider prescribes it. And avoid caffeine in the evening, as this can disrupt sleep. Caffeine is in drinks such as soda, tea, and coffee, but it is in some foods like chocolate too.

CHAPTER FOUR

HOW DO I TAKE MY GAME TO
THE NEXT LEVEL?

Belgian soccer player Romelu Lukaku began playing organized soccer around age six. He remembers, "When I was five there was the World Cup '98 going on. In Belgium at the time, we could always start soccer from six years old. So, basically what my dad did, he recorded all the goals that were scored and he would play the videos every other day. And I would watch it with my brother over and over and over again. At one point you start memorizing the actions and the goals. So, basically I would watch Ronaldo . . . and then when I was six I played for my first team which was called Rupel Boom. It's a team in the neighborhood where I grew up."[49]

For Lukaku, those World Cup '98 videos and his neighborhood team, Rupel Boom, were the first steps on the path to becoming the player he is now. Lukaku plays for Manchester United FC in the English Premier League and the Belgian men's national team. He competed in the 2018 FIFA World Cup in Russia, netting four goals and helping the Belgian team take home a bronze medal.

All players who play at the highest levels begin with a dream and a neighborhood team. So what does it take for a player competing with a club team or a high school team to make it to the next levels of soccer competition?

Romelu Lukaku has played soccer at the highest level. He has been a soccer player for most of his life.

For many high school players, the goal might be to play soccer at the college level. Next College Student Athlete (NCSA), a college athletic recruiting network, reports that 9.6 percent of female high school soccer players go on to play at the college level, and about 2.3 percent of them play at a Division I school. For males, about 7.9 percent of high school players compete in college, with about 1.1 percent of them playing at a Division I school. The statistics show that the competition for moving from high school soccer to college level soccer is steep. But there are things a player can do to improve his or her chances of making that leap to a college team.

BUILDING ON HIGH SCHOOL SKILLS

A high school soccer player hoping to play soccer at the college level should continue to work on many of the same technical skills used at the high school level. Players can use ball control drills to help refine their first touch and ball control skills. High school players might have the skills to trap the ball. But at the college level, the game moves faster and is more physical.

> **"So [we] look for how fast can a player move the ball and, on the other side of it, how fast can a player move off the ball."**[50]
>
> – *Chris Bergmann, Virginia Military Institute women's head coach*

"If your touch gets away from you and it takes a couple of steps to get it, it's going to slow the pace down," says Chris Bergmann, the head coach of the women's soccer team at Virginia Military Institute. "Tempo is extremely important to us. So [we] look for how fast can a player move the ball and, on the other side of it, how fast can a player move off the ball. After a pass, do you watch it, or do you move?"[50] Coaches want to see high school players who are alert and aware of the play unfolding, and who then make the first touch headed in the right direction.

PASSING LONG AND SHORT

Players should also focus on drills that help strengthen both their long and short passes. Coaches recruiting for college will want to know a player's ability to pass at longer distances. Even defenders need to have strong passing skills at the college level.

Matt Gill is the head coach of Huntingdon College women's soccer team. His team plays with three defenders using a 3-4-1-2 formation. This is a formation with three defenders, four midfielders (two center and two wingers), one center midfielder playing farther forward, and two forwards. For Gill, it is important that his defenders can defend well in one-on-one situations, but they also need to be able to launch an attack by making the right pass. "Possession out of the back is huge with the three-back system," Gill says. "If you lose it deep in your defensive third then you'll be countered quickly. So we're looking for players with composure."[51]

SHOOTING AND FINISHING

A high school player with strong shooting and finishing skills might also catch the attention of college coaches. Shooting usually refers to shots taken some distance away from the goal. Finishing is when players are close to the goal and score off a ball passed in to them. While a player can practice shooting alone, to practice finishing, at least two players are needed—one to pass and the other to score. The key to getting better at finishing is simply repetition. By practicing many repetitions of finishing, a player improves his or her technique and gains confidence for success in finishing in game situations.

With the increased speed and toughness of the college game, coaches are looking for players who can keep up with this more intense level of play. "It's great if you're a technical player, but if you can't handle the physical demands of the

> "It's great if you're a technical player, but if you can't handle the physical demands of the game at the end of the day it's going to be really hard, especially at the Division I level."[52]
>
> – Chris Haught-Thompson, Knox College women's head coach

game at the end of the day it's going to be really hard, especially at the Division I level," says Chris Haught-Thompson.[52] He was the women's assistant coach at Virginia Military Institute and later became the women's head coach at Knox College, a Division III school.

A player's size matters in the more physical college-level game, but coaches also look at other factors. "If you win the space, you'll win the ball," says Haught-Thompson. "Do you have the strength, the leverage, the smarts to win the space? It's the ability to read the game well and getting to the spot before a bigger player who will likely win the 50-50 ball. If you get there first, it doesn't really matter how big you are. You need to use the tools that you have to make yourself successful."[53]

WELL-ROUNDED PLAYERS

College coaches are also looking for well-rounded, complete players. "Other than goalkeeping, we're not looking for position-specific players," says Mike Van Horn, who coaches the Bridgewater College women's team. "We're looking for a good soccer player. If she has the athletic ability, the technical ability, and can make good decisions, then hopefully she can move around to different places on the field."[54]

While a player may have played one certain position on the high school team or club team, a college coach may or may not use the player at that same position on the college team. "We're not necessarily recruiting for positions," says Chris Bergmann. "We're looking for the assets and the tools a player has and if that player can fit in our system."[55]

Nick Carter, who has coached at the collegiate level, stresses the importance of players with well-rounded skills. "We look for complete players," he says. "Sure, sometimes you see kids and it's obvious they

Players can do drills to improve their speed and agility. Drills often focus on speed and how to apply it during games.

have a certain position. But if you have the confidence to go one on one offensively, and handle one on one defensively, then you'll fit in anywhere on the pitch."[56]

IN SEARCH OF THE EXCEPTIONAL PLAYER

Players should keep working to develop their skills and be as ready as possible to catch the attention of a college coach. Chris Ducar is a coach with the University of North Carolina women's soccer team. He describes what he looks for in a high school player. "For us to notice any player, we have to see something exceptional," Ducar says.

"You have to possess an exceptional quality that makes you stand out against everyone on the field. Speed is something you can't teach and can be so hard to defend. If we see a player flying all over the field, that will attract our attention. Heading plays a huge role in the women's game, so if we see a young player dominating the air with combative heading, that's something that will get our attention. And lastly, a young lady that is just super skillful in all phases of the game is going to make us take notice. Ideally, we'd like to recruit the unicorn that has every one of those qualities!"[57]

> "We want to know how you're going to respond to a little criticism if you're on the field and we're trying to critique you a little bit."[59]
>
> – Matt Gill, head coach for the Huntingdon College women's soccer team

COACHES SAY CHARACTER COUNTS

"First, we're looking for character," says Chris Bergmann. "Character is refined through work ethic, how you treat the authority figures on the field, through how you treat your teammates. And then, ultimately, you see it through adversity, when things don't go your way."[58]

Coaches recruiting college players look for things like how a player responds to a teammate's mistake, or if a player rolls his or her eyes in response to a coach's instruction. With competition for landing a spot on a college roster being so stiff, players need to take advantage of every opportunity to make a positive impression on any college coaches who might be watching them.

"It's important," says Matt Gill. "We want to know how you're going to respond to a little criticism if you're on the field and we're trying to critique you a little bit. Basically, how coachable are you?"[59]

College coaches are looking for high school players who interact in a positive way with both their coaches and teammates. "Attitude is huge," says Nick Carter. "You can see who is coachable straight away just by how they interact with the coach, and even how they interact with their parents after the games."[60]

COUNTDOWN TO COLLEGE

High school soccer players should not wait until their senior year to start thinking about college and the dream of being recruited to play at that level. A high school player's first step might be a conversation with his or her high school or club team coach, asking the coach's opinion of his or her skill level and ability to play college-level soccer. A high school coach might also be able to suggest a range of schools where the player might have a chance of making the team. There are college soccer teams at the Division I, Division II, Division III, National Association of Intercollegiate Athletics, and junior college level.

COLLEGE RECRUITING TIMELINE

Schellas Hyndman was a highly successful college coach at Southern Methodist University and also the head coach at the MLS's FC Dallas. He later became head coach at Grand Canyon University. Hyndman has a suggested timeline for high school players. In the sophomore year players should start thinking about potential colleges. In junior year, make a list of five or six colleges and research these schools. Players should visit each school and look for opportunities to meet players and coaches or attend a camp at each school. By senior year, players should narrow their list down to three or four schools. They should also be open to any schools that might reach out to contact them.

Student athletes are still students. Players have to balance class, practices, games, workouts, and their social life.

Players should do their homework on any potential schools on their list. Take into consideration the school as a whole package. Think about academics, athletics, scholarships, social life, and distance from home. Players should also make time to learn about the National Collegiate Athletics Association (NCAA) rules for recruiting. Players can enlist the help of their high school coaches. Coaches want to see their players succeed, and often they can be a big help in navigating the recruiting process.

Hyndman offers these words of advice to high school players: "Would you come to this university if you didn't make the soccer team? If the answer is no, don't go to that university. If you would go to the university even if you didn't make the team, this could be the right university for you. Enjoy this time, investigate and prepare yourself to make the right decision. It will be one of the biggest decisions of your life."[61]

DON'T FORGET ABOUT THE GRADES

It could be easy for high school players to focus all their energy on their soccer game in hopes of being recruited by a college coach. But the academics matter too. High school players must aim for their best work in the classroom.

"Players forget this," says Hyndman. "A lot of people think that just because they're athletes someone will bend the rules or give them a break. The NCAA is very concerned about student athletes, academics and graduation rates. Today there is more pressure on coaches to makes sure their student athletes graduate. Why would a coach recruit a player that has bad grades when it could affect the coaches' number of scholarships or job stability?"[62] College coaches will be looking at a high school player's grades and test scores on the ACT or SAT.

> **"Why would a coach recruit a player that has bad grades when it could affect the coaches' number of scholarships or job stability?"[62]**
>
> – Schellas Hyndman, Grand Canyon University men's head coach

PROFESSIONAL SOCCER LEAGUES

In North America, MLS for men and NWSL for women are the highest level professional soccer leagues. MLS teams play from March until November or December. NWSL teams play from March through September. In Europe there are many professional soccer leagues, but the "Big Five" are England's Premier League, Spain's La Liga, Germany's Bundesliga, Italy's Serie A, and France's Ligue 1. Most of the European leagues play a season that runs from August through May.

Beyond the regular season, many European teams compete in highly popular Europe-wide tournaments. One big difference between MLS teams and European teams is that in Europe when a team performs poorly during a season, they can be moved down to a lower division of play. Teams playing well in the lower divisions have a chance to move to a higher division. This is called relegation.

YOUTH SOCCER DEVELOPMENT

Another big difference between MLS and European soccer is the way that young soccer players are developed. In the United States, soccer players develop their skills mainly by playing for high school, club, and college teams. In Europe, the professional teams sign players at a very young age and then bring them into the teams' youth academies to develop their skills and mature them as soccer players. Players successful in advancing through the youth academy system develop superb technical skills, preparing them to play at the professional level.

Following the European model, MLS teams began development academies in 2007. The arrival of these academies in the United States helped boost the development of American soccer talent. But the academies are still growing to their full potential, with some MLS

CLUB TEAM VS. HIGH SCHOOL TEAM

Should a high school player hoping to be recruited for college soccer play for his or her high school team or for a club team? A recent NCAA survey of 21,233 college athletes showed that among soccer players, 93 percent of men and 95 percent of women played for a club soccer team. Many played for both a club and local high school team. When playing for a high school, they get to play many games with their family, friends, and school community cheering them on. High school teams also give players a chance to mature into leadership roles as they move from freshman toward senior year. On the other hand, club teams usually offer players a chance for higher level competition than is found at the local high school games. The NCSA college athletic recruiting network recommends that high school athletes, especially males, should play at least two years with a club team to improve their chances of being recruited by a college. The club teams usually train year-round and have access to high-quality facilities with highly trained coaches. Each player must decide, based on his or her skill level and goals as far as college-level soccer, whether to play high school soccer, club soccer, or both.

teams having much stronger programs than other teams. As time passes, the MLS academies are becoming more important in their role of developing soccer talent. In general, when many American players are just starting to play college soccer around eighteen years old, the European players are already playing at a highly competitive level of soccer.

NEXT STEPS TO THE PROS

Players in the United States who dream of playing professionally usually follow several routes toward the professional leagues. The first step is to play for a very competitive club team or travel team. The US

WORLD CUP COMPETITION

The FIFA World Cup is the biggest single-event sporting competition in the world. The competition draws the top men's national soccer teams from the 211 countries that are part of FIFA. The World Cup is played every four years. The competition begins with the qualification phase, called the Preliminary Competition. This phase takes place over a three-year period to determine which national teams advance to take part in what is called the Final Competition. Out of the 211 FIFA member countries, thirty-one teams advance to play in the month-long final competition phase. Brazil is the only country to have played in every World Cup tournament, and it has won five World Cup titles. Italy, Germany, Argentina, Uruguay, France, England, and Spain have all won at least one title. France won the 2018 World Cup, which was played in Russia.

Soccer Development Academy and Elite Clubs National League are two top-level leagues for club teams. Playing for an MLS Academy youth team is also a great opportunity for a player to be noticed. These academies give players easier access to professional coaches.

US Youth Soccer's Olympic Development Program (ODP) is another way outstanding players can gain access to high-level competition. Players are chosen for the program through tryouts at the state level. The best players from each age-group form a national team that competes in international competition. Playing with an ODP team gives a player the chance for quality competition and exposure to regional and national team coaches and college coaches.

Getting recruited for college soccer is a big step toward the goal of playing professional soccer. Professional coaches scout for players from the best college teams. College players who do not get signed in the MLS or NWSL draft can try to attract a team's attention by attending a paid pro tryout or combine. MLS and NWSL both have tryouts.

Roster spots on professional teams are limited, and competition for those spots is fierce. But some see their dreams fulfilled at the highest levels of soccer competition. David Alaba is an Austrian player who plays for the German team FC Bayern Munich and also the Austrian national team. Alaba says, "You should always do what you love and if your heart is in it anything is possible."[63]

No matter how far soccer may take a player, it is good to remember that soccer is simply a game. Players must work hard, but they should also remember the joy of playing the game when they first experienced it as children. Steve Locker played college soccer at Penn State University, then later with the Hannover 96 team in Germany, and he has also coached college soccer. Locker says, "Before kids can play like a pro they must enjoy playing the game like a kid."[64] Players should always strive to hold on to the joy of playing the game.

SOURCE NOTES

INTRODUCTION: THE MOST POPULAR SPORT IN THE WORLD

1. Pelé and Robert L. Fish, *My Life and the Beautiful Game: The Autobiography of Pele*. Garden City, NY: Doubleday, 1977.

2. Roger Bennett, "Social Poet Captures the Beautiful Game," *ESPN*, October 9, 2013. http://www.espn.com.

3. Quoted in "David Beckham Pays Tribute to Legendary Pelé," *People*, March 20, 2008. https://people.com.

4. "Alex Morgan Quotes," *SuccessStory*, n.d. https://successstory.com.

5. Steve Mueller, "The 65 Most Inspirational Soccer Quotes," *Planet of Success*, July 1, 2017. www.planetofsuccess.com.

CHAPTER ONE: HOW DO I MAKE THE SOCCER TEAM?

6. Quoted in "The Story of Pelé in Life, in Art," *Sportslens*, December 12, 2011, https://sportslens.com.

7. Quoted in Andy Frye, "World Cup 2018 Interview with Landon Donovan," *Forbes*, June 18, 2018. www.forbes.com.

8. Quoted in Matt Law, "Tottenham Hotspur Striker Harry Kane Says Second-Season Syndrome Holds No Worries for Him," *Telegraph*, August 7, 2015. www.telegraph.co.uk.

9. Mike Woitalla, "Mia Hamm's Advice for Girls, Parents and Coaches," *Soccer America*, April 11, 2012. www.socceramerica.com.

10. Michael Clarke, "Interview with Pro Soccer Player Josh Smith," *Active Team Sports*. www.active.com.

11. Quoted in "Passion," *PassItOn.com*. www.passiton.com.

12. Dave Clarke, "Exclusive Interview: An Example of Coaching Excellence," *Soccer Coach Weekly*. www.soccercoachweekly.net.

13. Quoted in Mueller, "The 65 Most Inspirational Soccer Quotes."

14. Quoted in Carey Schumacher, "How to Shine at Soccer Tryouts," *Soccer Today*, December 10, 2014. www.soccertoday.com.

15. Quoted in Schumacher, "How to Shine at Soccer Tryouts."

CHAPTER TWO: HOW DO I GET MY BODY READY FOR THE GAME?

16. Nick Humphries, "Is the 10,000 Hour Rule True? Expert Advice from Retired MLS Defender Jimmy Conrad," *Train Effective*, 2017. http://blog.traineffective.com.

17. Quoted in Humphries, "Is the 10,000 Hour Rule True? Expert Advice from Retired MLS Defender Jimmy Conrad."

18. Quoted in Matthew Jussim, "Soccer Strength: 9 Exercises That Will Help Add Power to Your Game," *Men's Journal*. www.mensjournal.com.

19. Quoted in Jussim, "Soccer Strength: 9 Exercises That Will Help Add Power to Your Game."

20. Quoted in Jussim, "Soccer Strength: 9 Exercises That Will Help Add Power to Your Game."

21. Quoted in Matthew Jussim, "Soccer Training: 3 Exercises to Strengthen Your Core and Lower Body," *Men's Journal*. www.mensjournal.com.

22. Quoted in Mike Woitalla, "Alex Morgan: 'I Stuck to My Dream,'" *Soccer America*, January 8, 2014. www.socceramerica.com.

23. Quoted in Morty Ain, "USWNT's Christen Press Talks Body Issue and Swedish Soccer," *ESPN*, June 22, 2016. www.espn.com.

24. Quoted in Nick Humphries, "How to Strength Train for Soccer Effectively," *Train Effective*, n.d. http://blog.traineffective.com.

25. "20 Questions with Soccer Star Amy Rodriguez!," *Teen Vogue*, June 2, 2010. www.teenvogue.com.

26. Quoted in Jen Ator, "Lightning Round with Team USA's Alex Morgan," *Women's Health Magazine*, August 7, 2012. www.womenshealthmag.com.

27. "20 Questions with Soccer Star Amy Rodriguez!"

28. Quoted in Wake Forest Baptist Medical Center, "Proper Eating Habits Can Help Young Athletes On and Off the Field," *ScienceDaily*, August 8, 2017. www.sciencedaily.com.

29. Gina Giannetti, "Eat to Compete: Nutrition Tips for Student Athletes," *University of Rochester Medical Center*, September 11, 2017. www.urmc.rochester.edu.

30. Giannetti, "Eat to Compete: Nutrition Tips for Student Athletes."

CHAPTER THREE: HOW DO I MENTALLY PREPARE FOR THE GAME?

31. Quoted in "Chalk Talk: Interview with D1 Soccer Player Kelsee Pottorff," *The Female Athletes Mission*, June 12, 2018. www.thefamblog.com.

32. University of Lincoln, "Mental Toughness: Why Reaching the Top in Soccer Is All in the Mind, Not the Feet," *ScienceDaily*, June 19, 2014. www.sciencedaily.com.

33. University of Lincoln, "Mental Toughness: Why Reaching the Top in Soccer Is All in the Mind, Not the Feet."

34. University of Lincoln, "Mental Toughness: Why Reaching the Top in Soccer Is All in the Mind, Not the Feet."

35. Quoted in Gary Mack & David Casstevens, *Mind Gym: An Athlete's Guide to Inner Excellence*. New York: McGraw-Hill, 2001, p. 24.

36. Quoted in Jeffrey I. Moore, "Inspirational Soccer Quotes from the Greatest Players in the World," *Everyday Power*. https://everydaypowerblog.com.

37. University of Lincoln, "Mental Toughness: Why Reaching the Top in Soccer Is All in the Mind, Not the Feet."

38. Quoted in Anthea Levi, "5 Quotes from Carli Lloyd's Memoir That Will Inspire You to Be Your Best," *Health*, September 26, 2016. www.health.com.

39. Shaun Dreisbach, "U.S. Women's Soccer Team: What Success Looks Like Now," *Glamour*, May 5, 2015. www.glamour.com.

40. University of Lincoln, "Mental Toughness: Why Reaching the Top in Soccer Is All in the Mind, Not the Feet."

41. Quoted in Humphries, "Is the 10,000 Hour Rule True? Expert Advice from Retired MLS Defender Jimmy Conrad."

42. Quoted in "Mental Training—Focus for Soccer Players," *Soccer Training Info*. www.soccer-training-info.com.

43. Quoted in Ain, "USWNT's Christen Press Talks Body Issue and Swedish Soccer."

44. "Ryan Giggs & Roy Keane: Yoga and Soccer," *Soccer Training Info*. www.soccer-training-info.com.

45. Quoted in R. Morgan Griffin, "Can Sleep Improve Your Athletic Performance?" *WebMD*, August 13, 2014. www.webmd.com.

46. Quoted in Griffin, "Can Sleep Improve Your Athletic Performance?"

47. Quoted in Griffin, "Can Sleep Improve Your Athletic Performance?"

48. Quoted in Jonny Cooper, "Alex Oxlade-Chamberlain: How to Prepare for a Big Game," *Telegraph*, October 9, 2014. www.telegraph.co.uk.

CHAPTER FOUR: HOW DO I TAKE MY GAME TO THE NEXT LEVEL?

49. Quoted in Emma Fierberg and Scott Davis, "What It Takes to Be a World Cup Soccer Player," *Business Insider*, August 15, 2018. www.businessinsider.com.

50. Quoted in Joe Dougherty, "What College Coaches Want in a Player," *Soccer Wire*, February 20, 2015. www.soccerwire.com.

51. Quoted in Dougherty, "What College Coaches Want in a Player."

52. Quoted in Dougherty, "What College Coaches Want in a Player."

53. Quoted in Dougherty, "What College Coaches Want in a Player."

54. Quoted in Dougherty, "What College Coaches Want in a Player."

55. Quoted in Dougherty, "What College Coaches Want in a Player."

56. Quoted in Dougherty, "What College Coaches Want in a Player."

57. Quoted in Ross Hawley, "Recruiting Column: Interview with North Carolina Women's Soccer Coach Chris Ducar," *USA Today High School Sports*, August 4, 2017. https://usatodayhss.com.

58. Quoted in Dougherty, "What College Coaches Want in a Player."

59. Quoted in Dougherty, "What College Coaches Want in a Player."

60. Quoted in Dougherty, "What College Coaches Want in a Player."

61. "Schellas Hyndman's Dos and Don'ts of College Recruiting," *US Youth Soccer*. www.usyouthsoccer.org.

62. "Schellas Hyndman's Dos and Don'ts of College Recruiting."

63. Quoted in "How to Be a Professional Footballer, by Some of the Best Players in the Game," *Guardian*. April 5, 2017. www.theguardian.com.

64. "Steve Locker," *Stevelocker.com*. www.stevelocker.com.

FOR FURTHER RESEARCH

BOOKS

Dan Abrahams. *Soccer Tough: Simple Football Psychology Techniques to Improve Your Game*. Birmingham, England: Bennion Kearny Limited, 2012.

Stuart A. Kallen. *Careers If You Like Sports*. San Diego, CA: ReferencePoint Press, 2018.

Alex Morgan. *Breakaway: Beyond the Goal*. New York: Simon & Schuster Books for Young Readers, 2017.

Grant Wahl. *Masters of Modern Soccer: How the World's Best Play the Twenty-First-Century Game*. New York: Crown Archetype, 2018.

INTERNET SOURCES

Bielefeld University. "Mental Training for Soccer Tactics." *ScienceDaily*. June 2016. www.sciencedaily.com.

Joe Dougherty. "What College Coaches Want in a Player." *Soccerwire.com*. 2015. www.soccerwire.com.

Gia Giannetti. "Eat to Compete: Nutrition Tips for Student Athletes." *University of Rochester Medical Center*. 11 September 2017. www.urmc.rochester.edu.

"Schellas Hyndman's Dos and Don'ts of College Recruiting." *US Youth Soccer*. 2018. www.usyouthsoccer.org.

Carey Schumacher. "How to Shine at Soccer Tryouts." *Soccer Today*. December 2014. www.soccertoday.com.

WEBSITES

Athnet

www.athleticscholarships.net

For a high school soccer player hoping to have a chance to land a college scholarship, this website is a helpful starting point in understanding the process.

National Federation of State High School Associations

www.nfhs.org

The NFHS is the national leadership organization for high school sports. This website provides information related to high school soccer.

National Soccer Coaches Association of America

ww2.nscaa.com

This website is directed to coaches, but it gives great information on basic soccer skills, rules of the game, and some basic tactics during game situations.

Soccer Training Info

www.soccer-training-info.com

This website gives players detailed information on skills and drills to help improve their soccer game.

United States National Soccer Team Players Association

https://ussoccerplayers.com

If a player is new to the game or wants to be sure to understand the fundamentals, this is a great source. It covers the basic rules, explains the field and the clock, and describes the positions.

INDEX

Abrahams, Dan, 44
Alaba, David, 69

basic soccer skills,
  dribbling, 8, 12, 16, 34
  heading, 12, 16, 17, 62
  passing, 8, 12–16, 26, 28, 50,
    58–59
  receiving, 8, 12–14
  shooting, 8, 12, 14–16, 31,
    33–35, 59
  tackling, 12, 15–16
Beckham, David, 6
Bergmann, Chris, 58, 60, 62
breathing exercises, 51, 53
Bundesliga, 66

Caffrey, Paul, 32–33
Carter, Nick, 60, 63
Chicago Fire, 31
Chivas USA, 28
club teams, 8, 10, 18, 32, 35, 56,
  60, 63, 66–68
coaches, 9, 16, 22, 24–27, 31–33,
  35, 37, 42–48, 58–65, 67–69
college, 9, 21, 28, 35, 57–69
combat sports, 35–36
community leagues, 8, 10
concussions, 16, 17
Conrad, Jimmy, 28–29, 50–51
Cooper Test, 35
Crocetti, Michael, 53

development academies, 66–67
Donovan, Landon, 10, 52
drills, 4, 13, 19, 26, 30, 33–34,
  53, 58
Ducar, Chris, 61

Elite Clubs National League, 68
English Premier League, 16, 24, 30,
  43, 53, 55, 56, 66
ESPN, 17

FC Barcelona, 47
FC Dallas, 63
Fédération Internationale de Football
  Association (FIFA), 21, 23, 48,
  56, 68
Football Association, the, 5
futsal, 50

Galeano, Eduardo, 5
Geier, David, 53–54
Giannetti, Gina, 38–41
Gill, Matt, 58–59, 62

Hamm, Mia, 17–19, 45
Harvey, Nick, 35–36
Haught-Thompson, Chris, 60
Hetherington, Nate, 26–27
high school, 8, 10, 19–21, 23, 26,
  35, 56–61, 63–66, 67
Houston Dynamo, 32
hydration, 40–41
Hyndman, Schellas, 63, 65

Ina, Chris, 37–38
interval training, 30

Jones, Mike, 27
Juventus, 32

Kaka, Ricardo, 50
Kane, Harry, 16–17
Kansas City Wizards, 28
Keane, Roy, 53

LA Galaxy, 10, 52
La Liga, 66
Leroux, Sydney, 25
Ligue 1, 66
Lloyd, Carli, 48
Locker, Steve, 69
Lukaku, Romelu, 56

Major League Soccer (MLS), 7, 10,
    28, 32, 63, 66–69
Manchester United, 6, 53, 56
meditation, 52–53
Messi, Lionel, 50
Morgan, Alex, 8, 33, 37
music, 51, 53
My Life and the Beautiful Game:
    The Autobiography of Soccer's
    Greatest Star, 5

National Athletic Trainers'
    Association, 54
National Collegiate Athletic
    Association (NCAA), 64–65, 67
National Federation of State High
    School Associations (NFHS),
    20–21
National Women's Soccer League
    (NWSL), 34, 48, 66, 68–69
Next College Student Athlete
    (NCSA), 57, 67
Nicholson, Kevin, 24–25
nutrition, 4, 8, 37–39

Olympic Games, 8, 17
Orlando Pride, 8, 25
Oxlade-Chamberlain, Alex, 55

Pelé, 5, 10, 34, 50
positions in soccer,
    defender, 13–14, 22, 24, 28,
        58–59
    forward, 22, 24, 30, 59
    goalkeeper, 13, 14, 21–22, 50, 60
    midfielder, 19, 22, 24–25, 30,
        58–59
Pottorff, Kelsee, 42
pregame routines, 8, 51
Press, Christen, 34, 49, 52

racquetball, 36
Rakitic, Ivan, 47
Reading FC, 35
relaxing, 44, 51–53
Rodriguez, Amy, 36–37
Ronaldo, Cristiano, 32, 50, 56

San Jose Earthquakes, 28
SC Hessen Dreieich, 18
scholarships, 64–65
Serie A, 66
Sky Blue FC, 48
sleep, 53–55
Smith, Joshua, 18–19
Southampton Academy, 35
Stoler, Felicia, 55
stretching, 26, 53

tennis, 36
Thornton, Jim, 54
Tottenham Hotspur, 16
travel teams, 8, 10, 67
Tsu' Chu, 5

United States National Soccer Team
    Players Association, 22
US Soccer Development Academy,
    67–68
US Youth Soccer's Olympic
    Development Program (ODP), 68
Utah Royals FC, 34, 36

Van Horn, Mike, 60

Webb, Jordan, 31–32
weight training, 30–33, 37
World Cup, 7–8, 10, 17, 25, 29, 31,
    48, 56, 68

yoga, 53

IMAGE CREDITS

ABOUT THE AUTHOR

Donna B. McKinney is a writer who lives in North Carolina. She spent many years writing about science and technology topics at the US Naval Research Laboratory in Washington, DC. Now she enjoys writing about topics ranging from science to sports for children and young adults. She has coached community league soccer teams and played adult league soccer.